Greatest Leadership Quotes

365 days to inspire more
Power, Confidence, and Success

Joe Tichio

Copyright © 2021 Joe Tichio
All Rights Reserved

ISBN: 9798599836421

CONTENTS

iv

INTRODUCTION

My first book, Greatest Inspirational Quotes, was inspired by my website with the same name. It's been several years and I have received countless messages of thanks and support for the website and book.

Since publishing Greatest Inspirational Quotes, I've gotten married to the most amazing woman and have had 2 beautiful children.

I have come to think of leadership as a gift and responsibility. Now more than ever our world needs inspired leadership. Leadership in business, government, health, education, and in our homes.

Each of us has the responsibility to develop our leadership skills and share our gifts with the world. If you are a parent, your children will thrive from strong leadership in the home. If you run a business, coach a team, teach a class, or organize events, success will be a direct reflection of your effectiveness as a leader.

The more effective you are as a leader, the more success you will have. Business will prosper, teams will win, and children will succeed.

Every day there are countless leadership opportunities, little
decisions you make and actions you take, that add up and bring you closer to success.

Being a leader is an essential part of developing as a human being. My hope is that this book of quotes can inspire you over the next 365 days to develop the leader within you.

I hope you feel the inspiration to shine brightly and express

these qualities in your life. The more you do, the more these qualities will become second nature and as that happens the better your quality of life will become.
The pages that follow are a collection of quotes I've used and love. They've been influential in my life and I know they can have a positive impact on yours too. These quotes will help boost your inner power, guide you to success, and build your confidence.

This book is yours to read as you wish, but I recommend you take the 365-day journey and go one quote at a time. Cultivate your leadership skills with these inspiring words. Allow them to take root deep in your spirit and express their hidden power.

Thank you,

Joe Tichio

HOW TO GET THE MOST OUT OF THIS BOOK

This book has been designed to work in several ways:

1. It's a 365 day journey that you can start at any time. Read one quote a day, and allow that quote to be your inspiration for the entire day. Write it down, carry it with you, and read it often. Take a few minutes 2 - 3 times a day to jot down any ideas, thoughts, and feelings you have about the quote. You will be amazed at what discoveries you can have with this process.

2. You may read this book from beginning to end like any other book.

3. You may pick a number from 1 - 365 and see which quote you have selected and use that quote to inspire your day, as a focus for meditation and journaling, or to provide guidance when facing a difficult situation.

4. Enjoy the book as a useful resource to the greatest collection of leadership quotes.

Note: The quotes in this book are collected from many sources and time periods. To respect the integrity of the authors' work, I have maintained the gender references as they were originally used. A quote may say he/him/his/man, but the quote is equally applicable to both genders and all people.

I made every reasonable effort to correctly attribute each quote to the original author, but in some cases, it was impossible to identify who first spoke or wrote a particular quote. In some instances, I gave credit to a more recent rendition of the quote, while in others I chose the classic version. In some cases, I could not clarify who actually originated a quote so those are attributed to unknown.

Some quotes have several similar derivations. To decide

which one to use I took the liberty of choosing the version that best fit the essence of the book and would connect with the majority of readers.

365 DAYS OF LEADERSHIP QUOTES

1.
A good leader inspires people to have confidence in the leader,
a great leader inspires people to have confidence in themselves.
Eleanor Roosevelt

2.
A leader has the vision and conviction that a dream can be
achieved. He inspires the power and energy to get it done.
-Ralph Lauren

3.
The greatest problem with communication is
we don't listen to understand.
We listen to reply.
When we listen with curiosity,
we don't listen with the intent to reply.
We listen for what's behind the words.
-Roy T. Bennett, The Light in the Heart

4.
Outstanding leaders go out of their way to
boost the self-esteem of their personnel.
If people believe in themselves,
it's amazing what they can accomplish.
-Sam Walton

5.
Leadership is a privilege to better the lives of others.
It is not an opportunity to satisfy personal greed.
-Mwai Kibaki, Kenyan politician

6.
A leader is one who knows the way,
goes the way and shows the way.
-John C. Maxwell

7.
Leaders must be tough enough to fight,
tender enough to cry, human enough to make mistakes,
humble enough to admit them,
strong enough to absorb the pain,
and resilient enough to bounce back and keep on moving.
-Jesse Jackson

8.
The great leaders are like the best conductors-
they reach beyond the notes to reach the magic in the player.
-Blaine Lee

9.
Leadership is doing what is right when no one is watching.
-George Van Valkenburg

10.
Pull the string, and it will follow wherever you wish.
Push it, and it will go nowhere at all.
-Dwight D. Eisenhower

11.
I have three precious things which I hold fast and prize.
The first is gentleness; the second is frugality;
the third is humility, which keeps me
from putting myself before others.
Be gentle and you can be bold;
be frugal and you can be liberal;
avoid putting yourself before others
and you can become a leader among men.
-Lao-Tzu

12.
Your role as a leader
is even more important than you might imagine.
You have the power to help people become winners.
-Ken Blanchard

13.
One quality of leaders and high achievers in every area
seems to be a commitment to ongoing
personal and professional development.
-Brian Tracy

14.
The function of leadership is to produce more leaders,
not more followers.
-Ralph Nader

15.
A boss creates fear, a leader confidence.
A boss fixes blame, a leader corrects mistakes.
A boss knows all, a leader asks questions.
A boss makes work drudgery, a leader makes it interesting.
A boss is interested in himself or herself,
a leader is interested in the group.
-Russell H. Ewing

16.
Leaders aren't born, they are made.
And they are made just like anything else, through hard work.
And that's the price we'll have to pay to achieve that goal,
or any goal.
-Vincent Lombardi

17.
Leaders who win the respect of others
are the ones who deliver more than they promise,
not the ones who promise more than they can deliver.
-Mark Clement

18.
A leader takes people where they want to go.
A great leader takes people
where they don't necessarily want to go,
but ought to be.
-Rosalynn Carter

19.
Treat people as if they were what they ought to be
and you help them to become what they are capable of being.
-Johann Wolfgang Von Goethe

20.
If your actions inspire others to
dream more, learn more, do more and become more,
you are a leader.
-John Quincy Adams

21.
The challenge of leadership is to
be strong, but not rude;
be kind, but not weak;
be bold, but not bully;
be thoughtful, but not lazy;
be humble, but not timid;
be proud, but not arrogant;
have humor, but without folly.
-Jim Rohn

22.
Management is doing things right;
leadership is doing the right things.
-Peter F. Drucker

23.
A leader leads by example, whether he intends to or not.
-John Quincy Adams

24.
Our chief want is someone
who will inspire us to be what we know we could be.
-Ralph Waldo Emerson

25.
Great leaders are almost always great simplifiers,
who can cut through argument, debate, and doubt
to offer a solution everybody can understand.
-General Colin Powell

26.
It is the nature of man to rise to greatness
if greatness is expected of him.
-John Steinbeck

27.
No executive has ever suffered
because his subordinates were strong and effective.
-Peter Drucker

28.
Outstanding leaders go out of the way
to boost the self-esteem of their personnel.
If people believe in themselves,
it's amazing what they can accomplish.
-Sam Walton

29.
A competent leader can get efficient service from poor troops,
while on the contrary an incapable leader
can demoralize the best of troops.
-General John J. Pershing

30.
Do not follow where the path may lead.
Go instead where there is no path and leave a trail.
-Ralph Waldo Emerson

31.
When things go wrong in your command,
start searching for the reason
in increasingly large circles around your own desk.
-General Bruce Clarke

32.
The pessimist complains about the wind.
The optimist expects it to change.
The leader adjusts the sails.
-John Maxwell

33.
The true mark of a leader
is the willingness to stick with a bold course of action
- an unconventional business strategy,
a unique product-development roadmap,
a controversial marketing campaign
- even as the rest of the world wonders
why you're not marching in step with the status quo.
In other words, real leaders are happy to zig
while others zag.
They understand that in an era of hyper-competition
and non-stop disruption,
the only way to stand out from the crowd
is to stand for something special.
-Bill Taylor

34.
What the pupil must learn, if he learns anything at all,
is that the world will do most of the work for you,
provided you cooperate with it
by identifying how it really works
and aligning with those realities.
If we do not let the world teach us,
it teaches us a lesson.
-Joseph Tussman

35.
Leadership is the art of giving people a platform
for spreading ideas that work.
-Seth Godin

36.
You are not here merely to make a living.
You are here in order to enable the world to live more amply,
with greater vision, with a finer spirit of hope and achievement.
You are here to enrich the world,
and you impoverish yourself if you forget the errand.
-Woodrow Wilson

37.
I learned that if you work hard and creatively, you can have
just about anything you want, but not everything you want.
Maturity is the ability to reject good alternatives
in order to pursue even better ones.
-Ray Dalio

38.
The greatest leader is not necessarily the one who does the
greatest things. He is the one that gets the people
to do the greatest things.
-Ronald Reagan

39.
One of the tests of leadership
is the ability to recognize a problem
before it becomes an emergency.
-Arnold Glasow

40.
A true leader has the confidence to stand alone,
the courage to make tough decisions,
and the compassion to listen to the needs of others.
He does not set out to be a leader,
but becomes one by the equality of his actions
and the integrity of his intent.
-Douglas MacArthur

41.
Treat people as if they were what they ought to be,
and you help them become what they are capable of being.
-Johann Wolfgang von Goethe

42.
The quality of a leader is reflected
in the standards they set for themselves.
-Ray Kroc

43.
Anyone can hold the helm when the sea is calm.
-Publilius Syrus

44.
True leadership lies in guiding others to success,
in ensuring that everyone is performing at their best,
doing the work they are pledged to do and doing it well.
-Bill Owens

45.
Becoming a leader is synonymous with becoming yourself.
It is precisely that simple and it is also that difficult.
-Warren Bennis

46.
There exist limitless opportunities in every industry.
Where there is an open mind, there will always be a frontier.
-Charles F. Kettering

47.
Don't listen to the naysayers.
Make sure that you're working your butt off.
Make sure that you have a very clear vision
of where you want to go.
Don't shoot for lower goals – shoot for the stars.
-Arnold Schwarzenegger

48.
Leaders think and talk about the solutions.
Followers think and talk about the problems.
-Brian Tracy

49.
A leader is best when people barely know he exists.
When his work is done, his aim fulfilled,
they will say: we did it ourselves.
-Lao Tzu

50.
A genuine leader is not a searcher for consensus,
but a molder of consensus.
-Martin Luther King Jr.

51.
Before you are a leader,
success is all about growing yourself.
When you become a leader,
success is all about growing others.
-Jack Welch

52.
Do not follow where the path may lead.
Go instead where there is no path and leave a trail.
-Harold R. McAlindon

53.
The good-to-great leaders
never wanted to become larger-than-life heroes.
They never aspired to be put on a pedestal
or become unreachable icons.
They were seemingly ordinary people
quietly producing extraordinary results.
-Jim Collins

54.
We desperately need more leaders
who are committed to courageous,
wholehearted leadership and who are self-aware enough
to lead from their hearts, rather than unevolved leaders
who lead from hurt and fear.
-Bene Brown

55.
Average leaders raise the bar on themselves; good leaders raise
the bar for others; great leaders inspire others to raise their
own bar.
-Orrin Woodward

56.
Don't be afraid to give up the good to go for the great.
-John D. Rockefeller

57.
Leadership is not magnetic personality,
that can just as well be a glib tongue.
It is not 'making friends and influencing people,' that is flattery.
Leadership is lifting a person's vision to higher sights,
the raising of a person's performance to a higher standard,
the building of a personality beyond its normal limitations.
-Peter F. Drucker

58.
The greatest leaders mobilize others
by coalescing people around a shared vision.
-Ken Blanchard

59.
Nearly all men can stand adversity,
but if you want to test a man's character, give him power.
-Abraham Lincoln

60.
No leader sets out to be a leader.
People set out to live their lives,
expressing themselves fully.
When that expression is of value,
they become leaders.
So the point is not to become a leader.
The point is to become yourself,
to use yourself completely –
all your skills, gifts and energies –
in order to make your vision manifest.
You must withhold nothing.
You must, in sum,
become the person you started out to be,
and to enjoy the process of becoming.
-Warren Bennis

61.
Leadership is an action, not a position.
-Donald McGannon

62.
A leader is one who sees more than others see,
who sees farther than others see,
and who sees before others see.
-Leroy Eimes

63.
I've learned that people will forget what you said,
people will forget what you did,
but people will never forget how you made them feel.
-Maya Angelou

64.
To handle yourself, use your head;
to handle others, use your heart.
-Eleanor Roosevelt

65.
A boss has the title,
a leader has the people.
-Simon Sinek

66.
Consensus: The process of abandoning all beliefs, principles,
values, and policies in search of something in which no one
believes, but to which no one objects; the process of
avoiding the very issues that have to be solved, merely
because you cannot get agreement on the way ahead. What
great cause would have been fought and won under the
banner: I stand for consensus?
-Margaret Thatcher

67.
I alone cannot change the world,
but I can cast a stone across the water
to create many ripples.
-Mother Teresa

68.
We cannot lead anyone farther
than we have been ourselves.
-John C. Maxwell

69.
Leading people is the most challenging and,
therefore, the most gratifying
undertaking of all human endeavors.
-Jocko Willink

70.
A leader is like a shepherd.
He stays behind the flock,
letting the most nimble go out ahead,
whereupon the others follow,
not realizing that all along
they are being directed from behind.
-Nelson Mandela

71.
A man who wants to lead the orchestra
must turn his back on the crowd.
-Max Lucado

72.
Exemplary leaders know that if they want to gain commitment
and achieve the highest standards,
they must be models of the behavior they expect of others.
- James Kouzes and Barry Posner

73.
The secret of leadership is simple:
Do what you believe in.
Paint a picture of the future.
Go there. People will follow.
-Seth Godin

74.
Whenever you see a successful business,
someone once made a courageous decision.
-Peter F. Drucker

75.
Be strong enough to stand alone,
smart enough to know when you need help,
and brave enough to ask for it.
-Unknown

76.
If your actions create a legacy
that inspires others to dream more,
learn more, do more and become more,
then, you are an excellent leader.
-Dolly Parton

77.
I am not a product of my circumstances.
I am a product of my decisions.
-Stephen R. Covey

78.
Leaders are not, as we are often led to think, people who go
along with huge crowds following them. Leaders are
people who go their own way without caring, or even
looking to see, whether anyone is following them.
"Leadership qualities" are not the qualities that enable
people to attract followers, but those that enable them to do
without them. They include, at the very least, courage,
endurance, patience, humor, flexibility, resourcefulness,
stubbornness, a keen sense of reality, and the ability to keep
a cool and clear head, even when things are going badly.
True leaders, in short, do not make people into followers,
but into other leaders.
-John Holt

79.
The best time to plant a tree was 20 years ago.
The second best time is now.
-Chinese Proverb

80.
Someone is sitting in the shade today
because someone planted a tree a long time ago.
-Warren Buffett

81.
Do not watch how other people walk their path
to success or try to keep up with them.
Do not give in to the herd instinct.
You have your own calling.
The majority take the roads well-trodden
but true success is achieved by the few
who refuse to follow the rule "do as I do"
and independently tread their own path.
-Vadim Zeland

82.
Be brilliant in the basics.
Don't dabble in your job; you must master it.
That applies at every level as you advance.
Analyze yourself. Identify weaknesses and improve yourself.
If you're not running three miles in eighteen minutes,
work out more;
if you're not a good listener, discipline yourself;
if you're not swift at calling in artillery fire, rehearse.
Your troops are counting on you.
Of course you'll screw up sometimes; don't dwell on that.
The last perfect man on earth died on a cross long ago –
just be honest and move on,
smarter for what your mistake taught you.
-Jim Mattis

83.
Do the difficult things while they are easy
and do the great things while they are small.
A journey of a thousand miles must begin with a single step.
-Lao Tzu

84.
We don't make movies to make money,
we make money to make more movies.
-Walt Disney

85.
Be willing to be uncomfortable.
Be comfortable being uncomfortable.
It may get tough,
but it's a small price to pay for living a dream.
-Peter McWilliams

86.
To be a great leader you have to care more, do more, and help
more. Your actions will set the tone for the entire team.
-Joe Tichio

87.
Leadership is lifting a person's vision to high sights,
the raising of a person's performance to a higher standard,
the building of a personality beyond its normal limitations.
-Peter F. Drucker

88.
The important thing is this:
to be able to give up in any given moment
all that we are for what we can become.
-Charles Du Bos

89.
A year from now you will wish you had started today.
-Karen Lamb

90.
For me life is continuously being hungry.
The meaning of life is not simply to exist, to survive,
but to move ahead, to go up, to achieve, to conquer.
-Arnold Schwarzenegger

91.
Throw yourself into some work
you believe in with all your heart,
live for it, die for it, and you will find the happiness
that you had thought could never be yours.
-Dale Carnegie

92.
I am not afraid of an army of lions led by a sheep;
I am afraid of an army of sheep led by a lion.
-Alexander the Great

93.
Leadership is not just about giving energy…
it's unleashing other people's energy.
-Paul Polman

94.
We treat our people like royalty.
If you honor and serve the people who work for you,
they will honor and serve you.
-Mary Kay Ash

95.
Great leaders are not defined by the absence of weakness,
but rather by the presence of clear strengths.
-John Zenger

96.
If the highest aim of a captain were to preserve his ship,
he would keep it in port forever.
-Thomas Aquinas

97.
You never change things by fighting the existing reality.
To change something, build a new model
that makes the existing model obsolete.
-Buckminster Fuller

98.
Leaders walk a fine line between self-confidence and humility.
-Stanley McChrystal

99.
Growing people and helping them to perform at high levels
is a key strategy for long-term success.
When employees grow, their productive capacity increases.
When their productive capacity increases,
the capacity of the organization increases –
it can do things better, or it can do things
it was not able to do before.
-Kent M. Keith

100.
It is literally true that you can succeed best
and quickest by helping others to succeed.
-Napoleon Hill

101.
The comfort zone is a nice place,
but nothing grows there.
Take the leap today and start your business!
-Caroline Cummings

102.
We cannot ask others to do what we have not done ourselves.
-Christiana Figueres

103.
Servant leadership pumps up the team with confidence,
which leads to high-performance.
-Marcel Schwantes

104.
I think leadership is service and there is power in that giving:
to help people, to inspire and motivate them
to reach their fullest potential.
-Denise Morrison

105.
Shine your light and make a positive impact on the world;
there is nothing so honorable
as helping improve the lives of others.
-Roy T. Bennett

106.
I just want to be right,
I don't care if the right answer comes from me.
-Ray Dalio

107.
Leaders are more powerful role models
when they learn than when they teach.
-Rosabeth Moss Kantor

108.
It's not the absence of leadership potential
that inhibits the development of more leaders;
it's the persistence of the myth
that leadership can't be learned.
This haunting myth is a far more powerful deterrent
to leadership development than is the nature of the person
or the basics of the leadership process.
-James Kouzes and Barry Posner

109.
Don't be intimidated by what you don't know.
That can be your greatest strength
and ensure that you do things differently from everyone else.
-Sara Blakely

110.
Leadership is the capacity to translate vision into reality.
-Warren Bennis

111.
When you put together deep knowledge about a subject
that intensely matters to you, charisma happens.
You gain courage to share your passion,
and when you do that, folks follow.
-Jerry Porras

112.
Individually, we are one drop.
Together, we are an ocean.
-Ryunosuke Satoro

113.
In your actions, don't procrastinate.
In your conversations, don't confuse.
In your thoughts, don't wander.
In your soul, don't be passive or aggressive.
In your life, don't be all about business.
-Marcus Aurelius

114.
All employees have an innate desire to contribute
to something bigger than themselves.
-Jag Randhawa

115.
I know of no single formula for success.
But over the years I have observed that
some attributes of leadership are universal
and are often about finding ways of encouraging people
to combine their efforts, their talents, their insights,
their enthusiasm and their inspiration to work together.
-Queen Elizabeth II

116.
Everyone talks about building a relationship with your
customer.
I think you build one with your employees first.
-Angela Ahrendts

117.
Communication is the most important skill
any leader can possess.
-Richard Branson

118.
So much of leadership ability is about
how other people experience themselves in your presence.
A great leader has a presence that makes other people bigger.
-Shane Parrish

119.
One of the toughest things for leaders to master is kindness.
Kindness shares credit and offers
enthusiastic praise for others' work.
It's a balancing act between being genuinely kind
and not looking weak.
-Travis Bradberry

120.
"Turned on" people figure out how to beat the competition,
"Turned off" people only complain
about being beaten by the competition.
-Ben Simonton

121.
Love the life you have while you create the life of your dreams.
Don't think you have to choose one over the other.
-Hal Elrod

122.
The sidelines are not where you want to live your life.
The world needs you in the arena.
-Tim Cook

123.
Connect the dots between individual roles
and the goals of the organization.
When people see that connection,
they get a lot of energy out of work.
They feel the importance, dignity, and meaning in their job.
-Ken Blanchard

124.
As a leader, it's a major responsibility on your shoulders
to practice the behavior you want others to follow.
-Himanshu Bhatia

125.
Ultimately, leadership is not about glorious crowning acts.
It's about keeping your team focused on a goal
and motivated to do their best to achieve it,
especially when the stakes are high
and the consequences really matter.
It is about laying the groundwork for others' success,
and then standing back and letting them shine.
-Chris Hadfield

126.
It is not the strongest of the species that survive,
nor the most intelligent, but the one most responsive to change.
-Charles Darwin

127.
Effective leadership is putting first things first.
Effective management is discipline, carrying it out.
-Stephen R. Covey

128.
The leaders who get the most out of their people
are the leaders who care most about their people.
-Simon Sinek

129.
A boss loves power; a leader loves people.
-Amit Kalantri

130.
A leader is not an administrator who loves to run others,
but someone who carries water for his people
so that they can get on with their jobs.
-Robert Townsend

131.
You can't sell it outside
if you can't sell it inside.
-Stan Slap

132.
Example is not the main thing in influencing others.
It is the only thing.
-Albert Schweitzer

133.
What you do is what matters,
not what you think or say or plan.
-Jason Fried

134.
It is much more powerful to get others to agree with you
through your actions, without saying a word.
Demonstrate, do not explicate.
-Robert Greene

135.
Leadership is practiced not so much in words
as in attitude and in actions.
-Harold S. Geneen

136.
Identify your problems,
but give your power and energy to solutions.
-Tony Robbins

137.
Consistency is the true foundation of trust.
Either keep your promises or do not make them.
-Roy T. Bennett

138.
Don't set your goals by what other people deem important.
-Jaachynma N.E. Agu

139.
Leadership is not about being liked –
it's about staying safe in tough times
and giving people a vision of
why what they're doing is important
so they can make a difference.
-Mike Abrashoff

140.
Become the kind of leader
that people would follow voluntarily,
even if you had no title or position.
-Brian Tracy

141.
It is not fair to ask of others
what you are unwilling to do yourself.
-Eleanor Roosevelt

142.
Humans are ambitious and rational and proud.
And we don't fall in line with people who don't respect us
and who we don't believe have our best interests at heart.
We are willing to follow leaders, but only to the extent
that we believe they call on our best, not our worst.
-Rachel Maddow

143.
If you talk to a man in a language he understands,
that goes to his head.
If you talk to him in his language,
that goes to his heart.
-Nelson Mandela

144.
I would rather try to succeed and fail
than try to do nothing and succeed.
-Og Mandino

145.
I was always looking outside myself
for strength and confidence,
but it comes from within.
It is there all the time.
-Anna Freud

146.
I do not think there is any other quality
so essential to success of any kind
as the quality of perseverance.
It overcomes almost everything, even nature.
-John D. Rockefeller

147.
The question isn't who is going to let me;
it's who is going to stop me.
-Ayn Rand

148.
Too many of us are not living our dreams
because we are living our fears.
-Les Brown

149.
We are what we pretend to be,
so we must be careful about what we pretend to be.
-Kurt Vonnegut

150.
The most fulfilled and effective people I know – world-famous
creatives, billionaires, thought leaders, and more – look at
their life's journey as perhaps 25 percent finding
themselves
and 75 percent creating themselves.
-Tim Ferriss

151.
If you hear a voice within you say, 'You cannot paint,'
then by all means paint and that voice will be silenced.
-Vincent Van Gogh

152.
To achieve something meaningful,
you need to know where you are heading
and be willing to train hard to get there.
-Arianna Huffington

153.
You get in life what you have the courage to ask for.
-Nancy D. Solomon

154.
The ultimate measure of a man
is not where he stands in moments of comfort,
but where he stands at times of challenge and controversy.
-Martin Luther King Jr.

155.
The supreme quality of leadership is integrity.
-Dwight D. Eisenhower

156.
Don't judge each day by the harvest you reap
but by the seeds that you plant.
-Robert Louis Stevenson

157.
The best executive is the one who has sense enough
to pick good men to do what he wants done,
and self-restraint enough
to keep from meddling with them while they do it.
-Theodore Roosevelt

158.
Build your own dreams,
or someone else will hire you to build theirs.
-Farrah Gray

159.
Things do not happen.
Things are made to happen.
-John F. Kennedy

160.
The most difficult thing is the decision to act,
the rest is merely tenacity.
-Amelia Earhart

161.
I never thought in terms of being a leader.
I thought very simply in terms of helping people.
-John Hume

162.
Who you are is defined
by what you're willing to struggle for.
-Mark Manson

163.
In order to live free and happily,
you must sacrifice boredom.
It is not always an easy sacrifice.
-Richard Bach

164.
The sum of our greatness lies not in asking
"what do I want to do?"
but rather "who do I want to be?"
-Lolly Daskal

165.
I'm not the bravest or smartest person,
but I'm courageous enough to dream big,
challenge myself and take bold risks.
-Richard Branson

166.
Don't follow the crowd,
let the crowd follow you.
-Margaret Thatcher

167.
Leadership is not a person or a position.
It is a complex moral relationship
between people based on trust, obligation,
commitment, emotion, and a shared vision of the good.
-Joanne Ciulla

168.
It takes 20 years to build a reputation
and five minutes to ruin it.
If you think about that, you'll do things differently.
-Warren Buffett

169.
Truly inspiring leaders get results by their own example:
They encourage others to be responsible and do the right
thing…they create space for others to be inspired and to
achieve their own greatness.
-Dr. Wayne Dyer

170.
Whatever you can do, or dream you can do, begin it.
Boldness has genius, power, and magic in it.
Begin it now.
-Johann Wolfgang von Goethe

171.
Good business leaders create a vision,
articulate the vision, passionately own the vision,
and relentlessly drive it to completion.
-Jack Welch

172.
We can do more than what we think.
It's a belief system that I have adopted
and it has become my motto.
There is more than meets the eye
and unless you are willing to experience new things,
you'll never realize your full potential.
-Wim Hof

173.
Some people dream of success,
while other people get up every morning
and make it happen.
-Wayne Huizenga

174.
Even in a crowded room,
likable leaders make people feel
like they're having a one-on-one conversation,
as if they're the only person in the room that matters.
And, for that moment, they are.
Likable leaders communicate
on a very personal, emotional level.
-Travis Bradberry

175.
If you do every job
like you're going to do it for the rest of your life,
that's when you get noticed.
-Mary Barra

176.
The truth of the matter is that
you always know the right thing to do.
The hard part is doing it.
-General Norman Schwarzkopf

177.
To do what you wanna do,
to leave a mark in a way that you think is important
and lasting, that's a life well-lived.
-Laurene Powell Jobs

178.
Wisdom equals knowledge plus courage.
You have to not only know what to do and when to do it,
but you have to also be brave enough to follow through.
-Jarod Kintz

179.
I do know one thing about me:
I don't measure myself by others' expectations
or let others define my worth.
-Sonia Sotomayor

180.
Treat a man as he is and he will remain as he is.
Treat a man as he can and should be
and he will become as he can and should be.
-Stephen R. Covey

181.
Leadership should be focused
on extending the ladder of opportunity for everyone.
-Justin Trudeau

182.
In order to remain relevant,
you must establish yourself
as a thought leader in your industry.
-Marc Benioff

183.
The hardest thing about being a leader
is demonstrating or showing vulnerability.
When the leader demonstrates vulnerability
and sensibility and brings people together, the team wins.
-Howard Schultz

184.
Many of life's failures are people
who did not realize how close they were to success
when they gave up.
-Thomas Edison

185.
If you have built castles in the air,
your work need not be lost;
that is where they should be.
Now put the foundations under them.
-Henry David Thoreau

186.
Risk more than others think is safe.
Care more than others think is wise.
Dream more than others think is practical.
Expect more than others think is possible.
-Claude Bissell

187.
When everything seems to be going against you,
remember that the airplane takes off against the wind,
not with it.
-Henry Ford

188.
Truly powerful people have great humility. They do not try to
impress, they do not try to be influential. They simply are.
People are magnetically drawn to them. They are most
often very silent and focused, aware of their core selves. ...
They never persuade, nor do they use manipulation or
aggressiveness to get their way. They listen. If there is
anything they can offer to assist you,
they offer it; if not, they are silent."
-Sanaya Roman

189.
Success is not the key to happiness.
Happiness is the key to success.
If you love what you are doing,
you will be successful.
-Albert Schweitzer

190.
Being a good listener
is absolutely critical to being a good leader;
you have to listen to the people who are on the front line.
-Richard Branson

191.
Leadership is about the team –
the culture they keep and embrace,
it's about empathy for your
customers, clients, employees
and the communities where you do business,
it's about doing the right thing for the right reasons,
being confident enough to take risks
and responsible enough to think of those
who your decisions and risks may affect.
-Kat Cole

192.
I think it's very important to have a feedback loop,
where you're constantly thinking about what you've done
and how you could be doing it better.
I think that's the single best piece of advice:
constantly think about how you could be doing things better
and questioning yourself.
-Elon Musk

193.
No one is less ready for tomorrow
than the person who holds the most rigid beliefs
about what tomorrow will contain.
-Watts Wacker, Jim Taylor and Howard Means

194.
I'm obsessed to extreme winners
because I think there's a madness to it.
I truly believe that in order to truly be great at something
you have to give into a certain amount of madness.
-Joe Rogan

195.
Just because most don't make it, doesn't mean you can't.
-Grant Cardone

196.
Being a good leader requires
remembering that you're there for a reason,
and the reason certainly isn't to have your way.
High-integrity leaders not only welcome
questioning and criticism,
they insist on it.
-Travis Bradberry

197.
Men make history and not the other way around.
In periods where there is no leadership, society stands still.
Progress occurs when courageous, skillful leaders
seize the opportunity to change things for the better.
-Harry S. Truman

198.
What I have learned is that people become motivated
when you guide them to the source
of their own power
and when you make heroes out of employees
who personify what you want to see
in the organization.
-Anita Roddick

199.
Leadership is developed daily, not in a day.
-Lolly Daskal

200.
The test of leadership is not to put greatness into humanity,
but to elicit it, for the greatness is already there.
-James Buchanan

201.
The very essence of leadership
is that you have to have a vision.
It's got to be a vision you articulate clearly and forcefully on
every occasion. You can't blow an uncertain trumpet.
-Reverend Theodore Hesburgh

202.
Leaders must get across the why as well as the what.
Their people need more than milestones for motivation.
They are thirsting for meaning,
to understand how their goals relate to the mission.
-John Doerr

203.
Leaders need to understand how profoundly they affect people,
how their optimism and pessimism are equally infectious,
how directly they set the tone
and spirit of everyone around them.
-Mike Abrashoff

204.
If you don't believe in yourself,
why is anyone else going to believe in you.
-Tom Brady

205.
The leader's unique legacy is the creation
of valued institutions that survive over time.
The most significant contribution leaders make
is not simply to today's bottom line;
it is to the long-term development of people
and institutions so they can adapt, change, prosper, and grow.
-James Kouzes and Barry Posner

206.
I think if you do something and it turns out pretty good,
then you should go do something else wonderful,
not dwell on it for too long.
Just figure out what's next.
-Steve Jobs

207.
Strength does not come from winning.
Your struggles develop your strengths.
When you go through hardships
and decide not to surrender,
that is strength.
-Arnold Schwarzenegger

208.
Take calculated risks.
That is quite different from being rash.
-George S. Patton

209.
Failing organizations are usually over-managed and under-led.
-Warren Bennis

210.
Strength is Happiness. Strength is itself victory.
In weakness and cowardice there is no happiness.
When you wage a struggle, you might win or you might
lose.
But regardless of the short-term outcome,
the very fact of your continuing to struggle
is proof of your victory as a human being.
-Daisaku Ikeda

211.
To know just what has to be done, then to do it,
comprises the whole philosophy of practical life.
-Sir William Osler

212.
It's the constant and determined effort
that breaks down all resistance
and sweeps away all obstacles.
-Claude M. Bristol

213.
Greatness is not a function of circumstance.
Greatness, it turns out, is largely a matter of
conscious choice, and discipline.
-Jim Collins

214.
Whatever you want to do, do it now!
There are only so many tomorrows.
-Pope Paul VI

215.
Leadership is not about titles, positions, or flow charts.
It is about one life influencing another.
-John C. Maxwell

216.
When something is important enough,
you do it even if the odds are not in your favor.
-Elon Musk

217.
It is impossible to be a maverick or a true original
if you're too well behaved and don't want to break the rules.
You have to think outside the box.
-Arnold Schwarzenegger

218.
Leaders should never be satisfied.
They must always strive to improve,
and they must build that mind-set into the team.
They must face the facts through a realistic, brutally
honest assessment of themselves and their team's
performance. Identifying weaknesses, good leaders
seek to strengthen them and come up with a plan to
overcome challenges.
-Jocko Willink

219.
Security is mostly a superstition.
It does not exist in nature,
nor do the children of men as a whole experience it.
Avoiding danger is no safer in the long run
than outright exposure.
Life is either a daring adventure, or nothing.
-Helen Keller

220.
To succeed you need to find something to hold on to,
something to motivate you, something to inspire you.
-Tony Dorsett

221.
Leadership is not about men in suits.
It is a way of life for those who know who they are
and are willing to be their best to create the life they want to
live.
-Kathleen Schafer

222.
Some of the greatest advances happen
when people are bold enough to speak their truth
and listen to others speak theirs.
-Ken Blanchard

223
Change is the province of leaders.
It is the work of leaders
to inspire people to do things differently,
to struggle against uncertain odds,
and to persevere toward a misty image of a better future.
-James Kouzes and Barry Posner

224.
Without leaps of imagination, or dreaming,
we lose the excitement of possibilities.
Dreaming, after all, is a form of planning.
-Gloria Steinem

225.
I'd rather be a could-be if I cannot be an are;
because a could-be is a maybe who is reaching for a star,
I'd rather be a has-been than a might-have-been, by far;
for a might have-been has never been,
but a has was once an are.
-Milton Berle

226.
Don't be afraid your life will end;
be afraid that it will never begin.
-Grace Hansen

227.
Abundance is not about
providing everyone on this planet
with a life of luxury-
rather it's about providing all
with a life of possibility.
-Peter Diamandis

228.
Most of the important things in the world
have been accomplished by people who have kept on trying
when there seemed to be no hope at all.
-Dale Carnegie

229.
Our emerging workforce is not interested in
command and control leadership.
They don't want to do things because I said so,
they want to do things because they want to do them.
-Irene Rosenfield

230.
Nothing can stop the man
with the right mental attitude from achieving his goal;
nothing on earth can help the man
with the wrong mental attitude.
-Thomas Jefferson

231.
Some people want it to happen,
some wish it would happen,
others make it happen.
-Michael Jordan

232.
Your time is limited,
so don't waste it living someone else's life.
Don't be trapped by dogma – which is living with the results of
other people's thinking. Don't let the noise of other's
opinions drown out your own inner voice. And most
important, have the courage to follow your heart and
intuition. They somehow already know
what you truly want to become.
Everything else is secondary.
-Steve Jobs

233.

WHAT MAKES A GOOD LISTENER?

Not interrupting.

Showing that you empathize: not criticizing, arguing, or patronizing.

Establishing a physical sense of closeness without invading personal space.

Observing body language and letting yours show you are not distracted, but attentive.

Offering your own self-disclosures, but not too many, or too soon.

Understanding the context of the other person's life.

Listening from all four levels: body, mind, heart, and soul.

-Deepak Chopra

234.
To be a leader, you have to make people want to follow you,
and nobody wants to follow someone
who doesn't know where he is going.
-Joe Namath

235.
Bet on your strengths.
It's an underrated business strategy
in a world where so many people are obsessed
with fixing their weaknesses
they give short shrift to the skills they were born with.
-Gary Vaynerchuk

236.
I am successful because I have never once believed
my dreams were someone else's to manage.
That's the incredible part about your dreams –
nobody gets to tell you how big they can be.
-Rachel Hollis

237.
The easiest thing to be in the world is you,
the most difficult thing to be
is what other people want you to be,
don't let them put you in that position.
-Leo Buscaglia

238.
The great leaders are not the strongest,
they are the ones who are honest about their weaknesses.
The great leaders are not the smartest;
they are the ones who admit how much they don't know.
The great leaders can't do everything;
they are the ones who look to others to help them.
Great leaders don't see themselves as great;
they see themselves as human.
-Simon Sinek

239.
Because the crew was convinced that I was 'on their team'
there were never any issues with negative criticism.
You as a mentor have to establish
that you are sincerely interested
in the problems of the person you are mentoring.
-Captain David Marquet

240.
If you're not failing, you're not pushing your limits,
and if you're not pushing your limits,
you're not maximizing your potential.
-Ray Dalio

241.
Time is neutral and does not change things.
With courage and initiative, leaders change things.
-Jesse Jackson

242.
Individual commitment to a group effort,
that is what makes a team work,
a company work, a society work,
a civilization work.
-Vince Lombardi

243.
Snowflakes are one of nature's most fragile things,
but just look at what they can do when they stick together.
-Vesta Kelly

244.
A brave leader is someone who says I see you.
I hear you. I don't have all the answers,
but I'm going to keep listening and asking questions.
-Bene Brown

245.
Experience is not what happens to you;
it is what you do with what happens to you.
-Aldous Huxley

246.
It seems like the world is crumbling out there,
but it is actually a great time in your life to get a little crazy,
follow your curiosity and be ambitious about it.
-Larry Page

247.
There's a silly notion that failure's not an option at NASA.
Failure is an option here. If things are not failing,
you are not innovating enough.
-Elon Musk

248.
Great leaders always seem to embody
two seemingly disparate qualities.
They are both highly visionary and highly practical.
-John C. Maxwell

249.
Always, bear in mind that your own resolution to succeed
is more important than any other one thing.
-Abraham Lincoln

250.
The miracle, or the power that elevates the few
is to be found in their perseverance
under the promptings of a brave, determined spirit.
-Mark Twain

251.
Too many talented people string and unstring their instruments
without ever playing their music.
-Unknown

252.
You see, in life, lots of people know what to do,
but few people actually do what they know.
Knowing is not enough!
You must take action.
-Anthony Robbins

253.
To practice leadership,
you need to accept that you are in the business of
generating chaos, confusion, and conflict.
-Ronald Heifetz

254.
You can't just sit there and wait for people
to give you that golden dream.
You've got to get out there
and make it happen for yourself.
-Diana Ross

255.
My own definition of leadership is this:
The capacity and the will to rally men and women
to a common purpose and the character
which inspires confidence.
-Bernard Montgomery

256.
To me, leadership is about encouraging people.
It's about stimulating them.
It's about enabling them to achieve
what they can achieve – and to do that with a purpose.
-Christine Lagarde

257.
Authentic leadership is about leading from the core
of who we are to inspire each of us to our best
contribution toward a shared mission.
-Henna Inam

258.
A determined soul will do more with a rusty monkey wrench
than a loafer will accomplish
with all the tools in a machine shop.
-Robert Hughes

259.
If you think you are too small to make a difference,
try sleeping with a mosquito.
-Dali Lama

260.
The starting point of great success and achievement
has always been the same.
It is for you to dream big dreams.
There is nothing more important,
and nothing that works faster
than to cast off your own limitations
and to begin dreaming and fantasizing
about the wonderful things
that you can become, have, and do.
-Brian Tracy

261.
The timeless in you is aware of life's timelessness;
and knows that yesterday is but today's memory
and tomorrow is today's dream.
-Kahlil Gibran

262.
Believe in yourself!
Have faith in your abilities!
Without a humble but reasonable
confidence in your own powers
you cannot be successful or happy.
-Norman Vincent Peale

263.
Far better it is to dare mighty things,
to win glorious triumphs,
even though checkered by failure,
than to take rank with those poor spirits
who neither enjoy much nor suffer much,
because they live in the grey twilight
that knows not victory nor defeat.
-Theodore Roosevelt

264.
Every problem has a gift for you in its hands.
-Richard Bach

265.
To accomplish great things,
we must not only act, but also dream;
not only plan, but also believe.
-Anatole France

266.
Victory becomes, to some degree, a state of mind.
Knowing ourselves superior to
the anxieties, troubles, and worries which obsess us,
we are superior to them.
-Basil King

267.
If I have the belief that I can do it,
I shall surely acquire the capacity to do it
even if I may not have it at the beginning.
-Mahatma Gandhi

268.
Do what you feel in your heart to be right,
for you'll be criticized anyway.
-Eleanor Roosevelt

269.
True leaders don't focus on getting more; they focus on giving more. Whether a parent, teacher, entrepreneur, or CEO – leadership is about focusing on how you can add more value by helping others to achieve their personal & professional objectives. The more people you help, the more influence, income, and opportunities you will attract, and the more successful you will become.
-Hal Elrod

270.
A person's success in life can usually be measured by the number of uncomfortable conversations he or she is willing to have.
-Timothy Ferriss

271.
The best way to predict the future is to create it.
-Peter Drucker

272.
A good leader doesn't get stuck behind a desk.
-Richard Branson

273.
When you can arrive at the point
where looking and listening
comes from your entire being,
you are setting the stage to be an inspiring leader.
-Deepak Chopra

274.
Talent wins games,
but teamwork and intelligence
wins championships.
-Michael Jordan

275.
The world is full of dreamers,
there aren't enough who will move ahead
and begin to take concrete steps to actualize their vision.
-W. Clement Stone

276.
You see things; and you say, "Why?"
But I dream things that never were;
and I say, "Why not?
-George Bernard Shaw

277.
The difference between the impossible
and the possible lies in a person's determination.
-Tommy Lasorda

278.
Let us not be content to wait and see what will happen,
but give us the determination to make the right things happen.
-Peter Marshall

279.
There comes a time in your life when you can no longer put off
choosing. You have to choose one path or the other. You
can live safe and be protected by people just like you, or
you can stand up and be a leader for what is right. Always,
remember this: People never remember the crowd; they
remember the one person that had the courage to say and
do what no one would do.
-Shannon L. Alder

280.
A leader should have higher grit and tenacity,
and be able to endure what the employees can't.
-Jack Ma

281.
Nothing in the world can take the place of persistence.
Talent will not; nothing is more common
than unsuccessful men with talent.
Genius will not; unrewarded genius is almost a
proverb. Education alone will not;
the world is full of educated derelicts.
Persistence and determination alone are
omnipotent. The slogan "press on" has solved and
always will solve the problems of the human race.
-John Calvin Coolidge

282.
I don't want other people to decide who I am.
I want to decide that for myself.
-Emma Watson

283.
Bring out the best in your team
by engaging them in the process.
The next time a team member encounters an obstacle,
instead of telling them what to do, ask them:
"how do you think we should handle this?"
-Joe Tichio

284.
If you want to be a leader whom people follow
with absolute conviction, you have to be a likable leader.
Tyrants and curmudgeons with brilliant vision
can command a reluctant following for a time,
but it never lasts.
They burn people out before they ever get to see
what anyone is truly capable of.
-Travis Bradberry

285.
Let us not become weary in doing good,
for at the proper time we will reap a harvest
if we do not give up.
-Bible, Galatians 6:9

286.
Four short words sum up
what has lifted most successful individuals
above the crowd: A Little Bit More.
They did all that was expected of them
and a little bit more.
-A. Lou Vickery

287.
Have goals so big your problems pale in comparison.
-Grant Cardone

288.
Leadership requires two things:
a vision of the world that does not yet exist
and the ability to communicate it.
-Simon Sinek

289.
Life is not about waiting for the storms to pass.
It's about learning how to dance in the rain.
-Vivian Greene

290.
If you are rich and powerful but unhappy,
what's the point of being rich and powerful?
-Thich Nhat Hanh

291.
Leadership is the ability to guide others without force
into a direction or decision that leaves them still feeling
empowered and accomplished.
-Lisa Cash Hanson

292.
We may be disappointed if we fail,
but we are doomed if we don't try.
-Beverly Sills

293.
Inaction breeds doubt and fear.
Action breeds confidence and courage.
If you want to conquer fear,
do not sit home and think about it.
Go out and get busy.
-Dale Carnegie

294.
In a battle between two ideas,
the best one doesn't necessarily win.
No, the idea that wins is the one
with the most fearless heretic behind it.
-Seth Godin

295.
It is often easier to make progress on mega-ambitious dreams.
Since no one else is crazy enough to do it,
you have little competition.
-Larry Page

296.
It is in the compelling zest of
high adventure and of victory,
and in creative action,
that man finds his supreme joys.
-Antoine de Saint-Exupery

297.
Anyone can give up, it's the easiest thing in the world to do.
But to hold it together when everyone else would understand
if you fell apart, that's true strength.
-Unknown

298.
If people believe you have a plan,
that you know where you are going,
they will follow you instinctively.
-Robert Greene

299.
Management is efficiency in climbing the ladder of success;
leadership determines whether the ladder
is leaning against the right wall.
-Stephen Covey

300.
Leadership is a potent combination of strategy and character.
But if you must be without one, be without the strategy.
-Norman Schwarzkopf

301.
The purpose of life is not to win. The purpose of life is to grow
and to share. When you come to look back on all that you
have done in life, you will get more satisfaction from the
pleasure you have brought into other people's lives than
you will from the times that you outdid and defeated them.
-Rabbi Harold Kushner

302.
The goal of many leaders is to get people to think more highly
of the leader. The goal of a great leader is to help people to
think more highly of themselves."
-J. Carla Nortcutt

303.
The first responsibility of a leader is to define reality.
The last is to say thank you.
In between, the leader is a servant.
-Max DePree

304.
Ten soldiers wisely led will beat a hundred without a head.
-Euripides

305.
Leadership is how to be, not how to do.
-Frances Hesselbein

306.
My research debunks the myth that many people seem to have .
. . that you become a leader by fighting your way to the top.
Rather, you become a leader by helping others to the top.
Helping your employees is as important as, and many times
more so than, trying to get the most work out of them.
-William Cohen

307.
We must be silent before we can listen.
We must listen before we can learn.
We must learn before we can prepare.
We must prepare before we can serve.
We must serve before we can lead.
-William Arthur Ward

308.
What are most people hungry for?
I believe it is spiritual and moral leadership.
Increases in technology, scientific inventions,
and medical miracles have been marvelous and incredible.
But we must use them properly to bring us joy,
and that requires spiritual and moral leadership.
-James E. Faust

309.
If leadership serves only the leader, it will fail.
Ego satisfaction, financial gain, and status
can all be valuable tools for a leader,
but if they become the only motivations,
they will eventually destroy a leader.
Only when service for a common good
is the primary purpose are you truly leading."
-Sheila Murray Bethel

310.
Leaders are not just born.
Sure, some people are born with strong
competencies and strengths for leading in certain
situations, but it is very clear that leadership can
also be developed. That means everyone can
strengthen their skills and abilities
to lead and influence.
-Dr. Susan Madsen

311.
Leadership is solving problems.
The day soldiers stop bringing you their problems
is the day you have stopped leading them.
They have either lost confidence that you can help
or concluded you do not care.
Either case is a failure of leadership.
-Colin Powell

312.
You've got to help others.
Don't just think about yourself.
Help others.
-Arnold Schwarzenegger

313.
To do great things is difficult;
but to command great things is more difficult.
-Friedrich Nietzsche

314.
Do not go where the path may lead,
go instead where there is no path and leave a trail.
-Ralph Waldo Emerson

315.
Associate yourself with men of good quality
if you esteem your own reputation;
for 'tis better to be alone than in bad company.
-George Washington

316.
More leaders have been made by accident,
circumstance, sheer grit, or will
than have been made by all
the leadership courses put together.
-Warren Bennis

317.
I'll tell you what leadership is, he said.
It's persuasion and conciliation and education and patience.
It's long, slow, tough work.
That's the only kind of leadership I know.
-Jim Mattis

318.
Your fears are not walls, but hurdles.
Courage is not the absence of fear,
but the conquering of it.
-Dan Millman

319.
Treating employees benevolently shouldn't be viewed
as an added cost that cuts into profits,
but as a powerful energizer that can grow the enterprise
into something far greater than one leader could envision.
-Howard Schultz

320.
Do not wait for leaders;
do it alone, person to person.
-Mother Teresa

321.
I attract a crowd, not because I'm an extrovert
or I'm over the top or I'm oozing with charisma.
It's because I care.
-Gary Vaynerchuk

322.
Only the weak are cruel.
Gentleness can only be expected from the strong.
-Leo Buscaglia

323.
A Boss:
Demands, Relies on Authority, Issues ultimatums, Says "I",
Uses people, Takes credit, Places the blame, Says "Go",
My way is the only way.

A Leader
Coaches, Relies on goodwill, Generates enthusiasm, Says
"We", Develops people, Gives credit, Accepts blame, Says
"Let's go", Strength in unity.

-Unknown

324.
There is one quality that one must possess to win,
and that is definiteness of purpose,
the knowledge of what one wants,
and a burning desire to possess it.
-Napoleon Hill

325.
Don't be afraid to give up the good to go for the great.
-John D. Rockefeller

326.
The fight is won or lost far away from witnesses
behind the lines, in the gym and out there on the road,
long before I dance under those lights.
-Muhammad Ali

327.
I cannot give you the formula for success,
but I can give you the formula for failure:
which is: Try to please everybody.
-Herbert B. Swope

328.
Successful leaders see the opportunities in every difficulty
rather than the difficulty in every opportunity.
-Reed Markham

329.
Leadership consists of nothing
but taking responsibility for everything that goes wrong
and giving your subordinates credit
for everything that goes well.
-Dwight D. Eisenhower

330.
We do not need magic to change the world,
we carry all the power we need inside ourselves already:
we have the power to imagine better.
-J.K. Rowling

331.
We are all faced with a series of great opportunities
brilliantly disguised as impossible situations.
-Chuck Swindoll

332.
There are moments in our lives when we summon the courage
to make choices that go against reason, that go against common
sense and the wise counsel of people we trust.
But we lean forward, nonetheless, because,
despite all risks and rational argument,
we believe that the path we are choosing is the right
and best thing to do.
-Howard Schultz

333.
Leadership is having a compelling vision,
a comprehensive plan, relentless implementation,
and talented people working together.
-Alan Mulally

334.
A good leader takes a little more than his share of the blame,
a little less than his share of the credit.
-Arnold Glasow

335.
Leadership is a verb.
It's a behavior, a lifestyle,
and part of who a person is.
We owe it to ourselves to live it
and expect the people in our community to represent it.
-Richard Branson

336.

7 Effective Ways to Make Others Feel Important

1. Use their name.
2. Express sincere gratitude.
3. Do more listening than talking.
4. Talk more about them than about you.
5. Be authentically interested.
6. Be sincere in your praise.
7. Show you care.

-Roy T. Bennett

337.
A person always doing his or her best
becomes a natural leader, just by example.
-Joe DiMaggio

338.
Leadership is not about a title or a designation.
It's about impact, influence and inspiration.
Impact involves getting results, influence is about
spreading the passion you have for your work,
and you have to inspire teammates and customers.
-Robin S. Sharma

339.
Mountaintops inspire leaders,
but valleys mature them.
-Winston Churchill

340.
Life's not about how hard of a hit you can give…
it's about how many you can take,
and still keep moving forward.
-Sylvester Stallone

341.
When I dare to be powerful-
to use my strength in the service of my vision,
then it becomes less and less important
whether I am afraid.
-Audre Lorde

342.
To understand the heart and mind of a person,
look not at what he has already achieved,
but what he aspires to.
-Khalil Gibran

343.
America would be a better place
if leaders would do more long-term thinking.
-Wilma Mankiller

344.
The time to repair the roof is when the sun is shining.
-John F. Kennedy

345.
Be who you are and say what you feel,
because those who mind don't matter
and those who matter don't mind.
-Dr. Seuss

346.
If a man knows not to which port he sails,
no wind is favorable.
-Seneca

347.
We never feel completely ready for life's big decisions;
but in taking the leap, we push ourselves to the next level.
-Patrick Bet-David

348.
At the center of your being
you have the answer; you know who you are
and you know what you want.
-Lao Tzu

349.
The most dangerous leadership myth is that leaders are born –
that there is a genetic factor to leadership.
This myth asserts that people simply either have
certain charismatic qualities or not.
That's nonsense; in fact, the opposite is true.
Leaders are made rather than born.
-Warren Bennis

350.
If you would not be forgotten,
as soon as you are dead and rotten,
either write things worth reading,
or do things worth the writing.
-Benjamin Franklin

351.
Love yourself, accept yourself, forgive yourself,
and be good to yourself
because without you the rest of us
are without a source of many wonderful things.
-Leo Buscaglia

352.
If you have a dream, don't just sit there.
Gather courage to believe that you can succeed
and leave no stone unturned to make it a reality.
- Roopleen Prasad

353.
If I have seen farther than others,
it is because I was standing on the shoulders of giants.
-Isaac Newton

354.
Set and maintain high standards.
If you have to be hard on people,
do it with love and a genuine wish for them to improve.
Praise people when they hit the standard.
-Sam Altman

355.
The lust for comfort
murders the passions of the soul.
-Khalil Gibran

356.
The mark of a great man
is one who knows when to set aside the important things
in order to accomplish the vital ones.
-Brandon Sanderson

357.
Whether you're 9 or 90,
stop trying to fix the things you're bad at,
and focus on the things you're good at.
-Gary Vaynerchuk

358.
We only get what we believe that we deserve.
Raise the bar, raise your standards
and you will receive a better outcome.
-Joel Brown

359.
The mediocre teacher tells.
The good teacher explains.
The superior teacher demonstrates.
The great teacher inspires.
-William Arthur Ward

360.
Leadership is much more an art,
a belief, a condition of the heart,
than a set of things to do.
-Max DePree

361.
The leader must explain not just what to do, but why.
It is the responsibility of the subordinate leader
to reach out and ask if they do not understand.
Only when leaders at all levels understand
and believe in the mission can they pass that understanding
and belief to their teams so that they can
persevere through challenges, execute and win.
-Jocko Willink

362.
If you want to change your life
you have to raise your standards.
-Tony Robbins

363.
The most effective way to do it, is to do it.
-Amelia Earhart

364.
As you enter positions of trust and power,
dream a little before you think.
-Toni Morrison

365.
You can be a leader in your workplace,
your neighborhood, or your family,
all without having a title.
-Travis Bradberry

Life is beautiful,
enjoy it!

- Much love,
Joe

INDEX

Greatest Leadership Quotes Book Index

1. Eleanor Roosevelt: wife of President Franklin D. Roosevelt. She was an advocate for civil rights, an international author, speaker, and politician.
2. Ralph Lauren: an American fashion designer, philanthropist, and billionaire businessman, best known for the Ralph Lauren Corporation.
3. Roy T. Bennett: author of The Light in the Heart. He loves sharing positive thoughts and creative insight.
4. Sam Walton: was an American businessman and entrepreneur best known for founding the retailers Walmart and Sam's Club.
5. Mwai Kibaki, Kenyan politician who was the third President of Kenya, serving from December 2002 until April 2013.
6. John C. Maxwell: American author, speaker, and pastor who has written many books, primarily focusing on leadership.
7. Jesse Jackson: an American civil rights activist, Baptist minister, and politician. He was a candidate for the Democratic presidential nomination in 1984 and 1988.
8. Blaine Lee: a founding Vice President of FranklinCovey and has been a contributing author to books by Stephen R. Covey and Norman Vincent Peale, and his book "The Power Principle: Influence with Honor" was published by Simon & Schuster in 1997.
9. George Van Valkenburg: I've come across this quote in several places attributing it to George Van Valkenburg, but unfortunately, I could not find any reliable information about this person.
10. Dwight D. Eisenhower: American politician and soldier who served as the 34th president of the United States from 1953 to 1961.
11. Lao-Tzu: philosopher of ancient China and best known as the author of the Tao Te Ching, a fundamental text of Taoism.
12. Ken Blanchard: has influenced the day-to-day management and leadership of people and companies throughout the world.
 His most successful book, The One Minute Manager, has sold over 13 million copies. Learn more www.kenblanchard.com

13. Brian Tracy: self-help author, motivational speaker, and business coach. Learn more at www.briantracy.com

14. Ralph Nader: American political activist, author, lecturer, lawyer, and presidential candidate, noted for his involvement in consumer protection, environmentalism and government reform causes.

15. Russell H. Ewing: a British journalist.

16. Vincent Lombardi: best known as the head coach of the Green Bay Packers during the 1960s. He led them to victory in the first two Super Bowls. Learn more www.vincelombardi.com

17. Mark Clement: I've come across this quote in several places attributing it to Mark A. Clement, but unfortunately I could not find any reliable information about this person.

18. Rosalynn Carter: Eleanor Rosalynn Carter is the wife of 39th President Jimmy Carter. Serving as the First Lady from 1977 to 1981, she was an envoy abroad and a leading advocate for numerous causes, including mental health research.

19. Johann Wolfgang Von Goethe: German poet, playwright, novelist, scientist, statesman, theatre director, critic, and amateur artist, considered the greatest German literary figure of the modern era.

20. John Quincy Adams: served as the sixth president of the United States, from 1825 to 1829.

21. Jim Rohn: entrepreneur, author, and motivational speaker. He developed programs to assist others to reach success in business and life. Learn more by visiting his website www.jimrohn.com

22. Peter F. Drucker: Austrian-born American management consultant, educator, and author.

23. John Quincy Adams: served as the sixth president of the United States, from 1825 to 1829.

24. Ralph Waldo Emerson: American essayist, lecturer, and poet who led the Transcendentalist movement in the mid 19th century. He is most famous for *Self-Reliance, The American Scholar*, and *Nature*.

25. General Colin Powell: an American politician, diplomat and retired four-star general who served as the 65th United States Secretary of State from 2001 to 2005.

26. John Steinbeck: Austrian-born American management consultant, educator, and author.

27. Peter Drucker: Austrian-born American management consultant, educator, and author.

28. Sam Walton: was an American businessman and entrepreneur best known for founding the retailers Walmart and Sam's Club

29. General John J. Pershing: John Joseph "Black Jack" Pershing GCB was a senior United States Army officer. He served most famously as the commander of the American Expeditionary Forces on the Western Front in World War I.

30. Ralph Waldo Emerson: American essayist, lecturer, and poet who led the Transcendentalist movement in the mid 19th century. He is most famous for *Self-Reliance*, *The American Scholar*, and *Nature*.

31. General Bruce Clarke: United States Army general, who served in World War I, World War II, and the Korean War.

32. John Maxwell: an American author, speaker, and pastor who has written many books, primarily focusing on leadership. Titles nclude: *The 21 Irrefutable Laws of Leadership* and *The 21 Indispensable Qualities of a Leader*.

33. Bill Taylor: an American diplomat, government official, and former soldier, who served as the 6th United States ambassador to Ukraine 2006 to 2009.

34. Joseph Tussman: was a philosophy professor at Cal Berkley and an educational reformer.

35. Seth Godin: American entrepreneur, author, and speaker. Learn more at www.sethgodin.com

36. Woodrow Wilson: who served as the 28th president of the United States from 1913 to 1921.

37. Ray Dalio: an American billionaire hedge fund manager and philanthropist who has served as co-chief investment officer of Bridgewater Associates since 1985. Author of *Principles: Life and Work.*

38. Ronald Reagan: served as the 40th president of the United States from 1981 to 1989.

39. Arnold Glasow: was a humorist and a successful American businessman

40. Douglas MacArthur: an American five-star general and

Field Marshal of the Philippine Army.

41. Johann Wolfgang von Goethe: German poet, playwright, novelist, scientist, statesman, theatre director, critic, and amateur artist, considered the greatest German literary figure of the modern era.

42. Ray Kroc: was an American businessman, joined McDonalds and help expand it into a global franchise. Also owned the San Diego Padres.

43. Publilius Syrus: a Latin writer, best known for his sententiae

44. Bill Owens: an American photographer, photojournalist, brewer and editor living.

45. Warren Bennis: was an American scholar, organizational consultant and author, widely regarded as a pioneer of the contemporary field of Leadership studies.

46. Charles F. Kettering: was an American inventor, engineer, businessman, and the holder of 186 patents.

47. Arnold Schwarzenegger: Austrian-American actor, businessman, former politician and professional bodybuilder. He served as the 38th Governor of California from 2003 to 2011.

48. Brian Tracy: a self-help author, motivational speaker, and business coach. Learn more at www.briantracy.com.

49. Lao Tzu: was an ancient Chinese philosopher and writer. He is the reputed author of the Tao Te Ching.

50. Martin Luther King Jr.: an American Christian minister and activist who became the most visible spokesperson and leader in the civil rights movement from 1955 until his assassination in 1968.

51. Jack Welch: was an American business executive, chemical engineer, and writer. He was Chairman and CEO of General Electric between 1981 and 2001.

52. Harold R. McAlindon: American Author, Writer, Management Speaker and Businessman.

53. Jim Collins: is a student and teacher of what makes great companies tick, and a Socratic advisor to leaders in the business and social sectors. He is the author of *Good to Great*, the #1 bestseller, which examines why some companies make the leap to superior results. Learn more at www.jimcollins.com

54. Bene Brown: an American professor, lecturer, author, and podcast host. Author of *Dare To Lead*.

55. Orrin Woodward: is a New York Times Best Selling Author and is listed as a top leadership expert and speaker for Inc Magazine.

56. John D. Rockefeller: was an American business magnate and philanthropist. He is widely considered the wealthiest American of all time, and the richest person in modern history.

57. Peter F. Drucker: Austrian-born American management consultant, educator, and author.

58. Ken Blanchard: has influenced the day-to-day management and leadership of people and companies throughout the world. His most successful book, The One Minute Manager, has sold over 13 million copies. Learn more www.kenblanchard.com

59. Abraham Lincoln: was an American statesman and lawyer who served as the 16th president of the United States from 1861 to 1865.

60. Warren Bennis: was an American scholar, organizational consultant and author, widely regarded as a pioneer of the contemporary field of Leadership studies.

61. Donald McGannon: was a broadcasting industry executive during the formative years of the television industry in the United States.

62. Leroy Eimes: author.

63. Maya Angelou: an American poet, memoirist, and civil rights activist. Author of *I Know Why the Caged Bird Sings*.

64. Eleanor Roosevelt: wife of President Franklin D. Roosevelt. She was an advocate for civil rights, an international author, speaker, and politician.

65. Simon Sinek: a British-born American author and motivational speaker. He is the author of five books, including *Start With Why*.

66. Margaret Thatcher: was a British stateswoman who served as Prime Minister of the United Kingdom.

67. Mother Teresa: honored in the Catholic Church as Saint Teresa of Calcutta, was an Albanian-Indian Roman Catholic nun and missionary.

68. John C. Maxwell: an American author, speaker, and pastor who has written many books, primarily focusing on leadership. Titles nclude: *The 21 Irrefutable Laws of Leadership* and *The 21 Indispensable Qualities of a Leader*.

69. Jocko Willink: a retired U.S. Navy SEAL officer, co-author of the #1 New York Times bestseller *Extreme Ownership: How U.S. Navy SEALs Lead and Win, Dichotomy of Leadership,* Podcast host, and co-founder of Echelon Front.

70. Nelson Mandela: was a South African anti-apartheid revolutionary, political leader and philanthropist who served as President of South Africa from 1994 to 1999.

71. Max Lucado: is an American author and pastor. Learn more at maxlucado.com

72. James Kouzes and Barry Posner: authors of The Leadership Challenge: How to Make Extraordinary Things Happen in Organizations

73. Seth Godin: American entrepreneur, author, and speaker. Learn more at www.sethgodin.com

74. Peter F. Drucker: Austrian-born American management consultant, educator, and author.

75. -Unknown

76. Dolly Parton: is an American singer, songwriter, multi-instrumentalist, record producer, actress, author, businesswoman, and humanitarian, known primarily for her work in country music.

77. Stephen R. Covey: American educator, author, speaker, and businessman. His most popular book was *The Seven Habits of Highly Effective People.* Learn more at www.stephencovey.com

78. John Holt, Teach Your Own: The John Holt Book Of Homeschooling

79. Chinese Proverb

80. Warren Buffett: an American investor, business tycoon, philanthropist, and the chairman and CEO of Berkshire Hathaway.

81. Vadim Zeland: Russian author of *Reality Transurfing.*

82. Jim Mattis: a retired United States Marine Corps general who served as the 26th US secretary of defense from January 2017 through January 2019. Author of *Call Sign Chaos: Learning to Lead.*

83. Lao Tzu: philosopher of ancient China and best known as the author of the Tao Te Ching, a fundamental text of Taoism.

84. Walt Disney: was an American entrepreneur, animator, writer, voice actor and film producer. A pioneer of the American

animation industry.

85. Peter McWilliams: was an American self-help author who advocated for the legalization of marijuana.

86. Joe Tichio: author, chiropractor, businessman.

87. Peter F. Drucker: Austrian-born American management consultant, educator, and author.

88. Charles Du Bos: was a French essayist and critic.

89. Karen Lamb: is a lecturer who teaches Oral Communication: Principles & Practices in the Oral Communication Program.

90. Arnold Schwarzenegger: Austrian-American actor, businessman, former politician and professional bodybuilder. He served as the 38th Governor of California from 2003 to 2011.

91. Dale Carnegie: author of *How to Win Friends and Influence People.* He was a writer, lecturer, and developer of self-improvement courses. Learn more at www.dalecarnegie.com

92. Alexander the Great: was a king of the ancient Greek kingdom of Macedon and a member of the Argead dynasty.

93. Paul Polman: a Dutch businessman, a former Procter & Gamble president for Western Europe, CFO of Nestlé and became vice president for the Americas.

94. Mary Kay Ash: Founder of Mary Kay Cosmetics.

95. John Zenger: a German printer and journalist in New York City. He printed The New York Weekly Journal.

96. Thomas Aquinas: was an Italian Dominican friar, philosopher, Catholic priest, and Doctor of the Church.

97. Buckminster Fuller: was an American architect, systems theorist, author, designer, inventor, and futurist.

98. Stanley McChrystal: a retired United States Army general best known for his command of Joint Special Operations Command.

99. Kent M. Keith: an American writer and leader in higher education.

100. Napoleon Hill: American self-help author of *Think and Grow Rich* which is among the 10 best selling self-help books of all time.

101. Caroline Cummings: Founder and CEO, Varo Ventures.

102. Christiana Figueres: is a Costa Rican diplomat with experience in high level national and international policy and multilateral negotiations.

103. Marcel Schwantes: is a speaker, executive coach, podcaster, and syndicated columnist

104. Denise Morrison: is an American business executive who served as president and chief executive officer of Campbell Soup Company.

105. Roy T. Bennett: author of The Light in the Heart. He loves sharing positive thoughts and creative insight.

106. Ray Dalio: an American billionaire hedge fund manager and philanthropist who has served as co-chief investment officer of Bridgewater Associates since 1985. Author of *Principles: Life and Work.*

107. Rosabeth Moss Kantor: is the Ernest L. Arbuckle professor of business at Harvard Business School.

108. James Kouzes and Barry Posner: authors of *The Leadership Challenge.*

109. Sara Blakely: is an American businesswoman, entrepreneur, and philanthropist. She is the founder of Spanx,

110. Warren Bennis: was an American scholar, organizational consultant and author, widely regarded as a pioneer of the contemporary field of Leadership studies.

111. Jerry Porras: is an American organizational theorist, Lane Professor Emeritus of Organizational Behavior and Change at the Stanford University Graduate School of Business. Co-author of the bestseller *Success Built to Last: Creating A Life That Matters*

112. Ryunosuke Satoro: was a Japanese writer active in the Taishō period in Japan. He is regarded as the "father of the Japanese short story".

113. Marcus Aurelius: was Roman emperor and a Stoic philosopher. He was the last of the rulers known as the Five Good Emperors,

114. Jag Randhawa: is a Technology Executive, Professional Speaker, Executive Coach, and award winning author of the book *The Bright Idea Box: A Proven System to Drive Employee Engagement and Innovation.*

115. Queen Elizabeth II: is Queen of the United Kingdom and 15 other Commonwealth realms.

116. Angela Ahrendts: is an American businesswoman who was previously the senior vice president of retail at Apple Inc. and

CEO of Burberry.

117. Richard Branson: is an English business magnate, investor, author and philanthropist.

118. Shane Parrish: was a cybersecurity expert at Canada's top intelligence agency and an occasional blogger. Learn more at fs.blog

119. Travis Bradberry: the co-author of Emotional Intelligence 2.0 and co-founder of TalentSmart, a San Diego provider of emotional intelligence tests and training, serving more than 75 percent of Fortune 500 companies.

120. Ben Simonton: Retired Captain US Navy after 26 years of service. Author of *Leading People To Be Highly Motivated And Committed*.

121. Hal Elrod: an American author, keynote speaker and success coach. He is the author of the bestselling books *The Miracle Morning* and *The Miracle Equation*.

122. Tim Cook: an American business executive, philanthropist and industrial engineer. Cook is the chief executive officer of Apple Inc., and previously served as the company's chief operating officer under its cofounder Steve Jobs.

123. Ken Blanchard: has influenced the day-to-day management and leadership of people and companies throughout the world. His most successful book, The One Minute Manager, has sold over 13 million copies. Learn more www.kenblanchard.com

124. Himanshu Bhatia: Himanshu "Sue" Bhatia: is the Chairman/Founder of IT and Business Services provider Rose International.

125. Chris Hadfield: a Canadian retired astronaut, engineer, and former Royal Canadian Air Force fighter pilot. The first Canadian to walk in space, Hadfield has flown two Space Shuttle missions and served as commander of the International Space Station.

126. Charles Darwin: was an English naturalist, geologist and biologist, best known for his contributions to the science of evolution.

127. Stephen R. Covey: American educator, author, speaker, and businessman. His most popular book was *The Seven Habits of Highly Effective People*. Learn more www.stephencovey.com

128. Simon Sinek: a British-born American author and

motivational speaker. He is the author of five books, including *Start With Why*.

129. Amit Kalantri: author of three books *I Love You Too, 5 Feet 5 Inch Run Machine - Sachin Tendulkar* and *One Bucket of Tears*.

130. Robert Townsend: an American actor, director, comedian, and writer.

131. Stan Slap: thought leader in how to achieve maximum commitment from manager, employee and customer cultures.

132. Albert Schweitzer: He was a theologian, organist, writer, humanitarian, philosopher, and physician.

133. Jason Fried: founder of 37signals, a privately held web-based software development company and the co-author of the international bestseller *Rework*.

134. Robert Greene: an American author known for his books on strategy, power, and seduction. He has written six international bestsellers: *The 48 Laws of Power, The Art of Seduction, The 33 Strategies of War, The 50th Law, Mastery, and The Laws of Human Nature.*

135. Harold S. Geneen: was an American businessman most famous for serving as president of the ITT Corporation.

136. Tony Robbins: one of the biggest names in the self help field. Robbins helps people transform the quality of their lives, become better leaders, and reach peak performance. To learn more visit his website www.tonyrobbins.com

137. Roy T. Bennett: author of The Light in the Heart. He loves sharing positive thoughts and creative insight.

138. Jaachynma N.E. Agu, author of *The Prince and the Pauper*.

139. Mike Abrashoff: Former Commander, USS Benfold and Author, *It's Your Ship.*

140. Brian Tracy: self-help author, motivational speaker, and business coach. Learn more at www.briantracy.com

141. Eleanor Roosevelt: wife of President Franklin D. Roosevelt. She was an advocate for civil rights, an international author, speaker, and politician.

142. Rachel Maddow: an American television news program host and liberal political commentator.

143. Nelson Mandela: was a South African anti-apartheid

revolutionary, political leader and philanthropist who served as President of South Africa from 1994 to 1999.

144. Augustine "Og" Mandino: American author who wrote the best-selling book *The Greatest Salesman in the World.* Learn more by visiting www.ogmandino.com

145. Anna Freud: the sixth and youngest child of Sigmund Freud, she followed the path of her father and contributed to the field of psychoanalysis.

146. John D. Rockefeller: was an American business magnate and philanthropist. He is widely considered the wealthiest American of all time, and the richest person in modern history.

147. Ayn Rand: is known for her two best-selling novels, *The Fountainhead* and *Atlas Shrugged*, and for developing a philosophical system she named Objectivism.

148. Les Brown: motivational speaker, author, former radio DJ, and former television host.

149. Kurt Vonnegut: an American writer who published fourteen novels, three short story collections, five plays, and five works of nonfiction.

150. Tim Ferriss: podcaster, investor, and author of: *The 4-Hour Workweek, The 4-Hour Body, The 4-Hour Chef, Tools of Titans, and Tribe of Mentors.*

151. Vincent Van Gogh: was a Dutch post-impressionist painter who is among the most famous and influential figures in the history of Western art

152. Arianna Huffington: is a syndicated columnist, a co-founder of The Huffington Post, and the founder and CEO of Thrive Global, and the author of fifteen books.

153. Nancy D. Solomon: The CEO and Founder of The Leadership Incubator, Nancy D. Solomon is an experienced and inspiring Leadership Keynote Speaker.

154. Martin Luther King Jr.: an American Christian minister and activist who became the most visible spokesperson and leader in the civil rights movement from 1955 until his assassination in 1968.

155. Dwight D. Eisenhower: American politician and soldier who served as the 34th president of the United States from 1953 to 1961.

156. Robert Louis Stevenson: was a Scottish novelist, poet and

travel writer, most noted for *Treasure Island* and *Strange Case of Dr Jekyll and Mr Hyde.*

157. Theodore Roosevelt: an American statesman, politician, conservationist, naturalist, and writer, who served as the 26th president of the United States.

158. Farrah Gray: an American businessman, investor, author, columnist, and motivational speaker.

159. John F. Kennedy: served as the 35th president of the United States.

160. Amelia Earhart: was an American aviation pioneer and the first female aviator to fly solo across the Atlantic Ocean.

161. John Hume: was an Irish nationalist politician, widely regarded as one of the most important figures in the recent political history of Ireland, as one of the architects of the Northern Ireland peace process.

162. Mark Manson: an American self-help author and blogger. Author of *The Subtle Art of Not Giving a Fuck.*

163. Richard Bach: an American writer widely known as the author of some of the 1970s' biggest sellers, including *Jonathan Livingston Seagull* and *Illusions: The Adventures of a Reluctant Messiah.*

164. Lolly Daskal: the founder of Lead from Within, a global leadership, executive coaching, and consulting firm based in New York City. Author of *The Leadership Gap: What Gets Between You and Your Greatness*

165. Richard Branson: is an English business magnate, investor, author and philanthropist.

166. Margaret Thatcher: was a British stateswoman who served as Prime Minister of the United Kingdom.

167. Joanne Bridgett Ciulla: is a pioneer in the field of leadership ethics as well as teaching and publishing on business Ethics.

168. Warren Buffett: an American investor, business tycoon, philanthropist, and the chairman and CEO of Berkshire Hathaway.

169. Wayne Dyer: was an American self-help and spiritual author and a motivational speaker. His first book, Your Erroneous Zones, is one of the best-selling books of all time.

170. Johann Wolfgang von Goethe: German poet, playwright,

novelist, scientist, statesman, theatre director, critic, and amateur artist, considered the greatest German literary figure of the modern era.

171. Jack Welch: was an American business executive, chemical engineer, and writer. He was Chairman and CEO of General Electric between 1981 and 2001.

172. Wim Hof: Wim Hof: is a Dutch extreme athlete noted for his ability to withstand freezing temperatures. He has set Guinness world records for swimming under ice and prolonged full-body contact with ice, and still holds the record for a barefoot half-marathon on ice and snow. Author, *Becoming the Iceman*

173. Wayne Huizenga: was an American businessman and entrepreneur. He founded AutoNation and Waste Management Inc.

174. Travis Bradberry: the co-author of Emotional Intelligence 2.0 and co-founder of TalentSmart, a San Diego provider of emotional intelligence tests and training, serving more than 75 percent of Fortune 500 companies.

175. Mary Barra: the chairman and CEO of General Motors Company. She is the first female CEO of a major automaker.

176. General Norman Schwarzkopf: was a United States Army general. While serving as the commander of United States Central Command, he led all coalition forces in the Gulf War.

177. Laurene Powell Jobs: Businesswoman and the founder of Emerson Collective. She is the widow of Steve Jobs.

178. Jarod Kintz: learn more at jarodkintz.com

179. Sonia Sotomayor: is an Associate Justice of the Supreme Court of the United States.

180. Stephen R. Covey: American educator, author, speaker, and businessman. His most popular book was *The Seven Habits of Highly Effective People*. Learn more www.stephencovey.com

181. Justin Trudeau: a Canadian politician who has served as the 23rd prime minister of Canada since 2015.

182. Marc Benioff: He is the founder, chairman and CEO of Salesforce

183. Howard Schultz: American businessman. He served as the chairman and chief executive officer of the Starbucks Coffee Company from 1986 to 2000, and then again from 2008 to 2017.

184. Thomas Edison: American inventor and businessman. He developed the phonograph, motion picture camera, and the light bulb.

185. Henry David Thoreau: American author, poet, philosopher, and leading transcendentalist. He is best known for his book Walden and essay Civil Disobedience.

186. Claude Bissell: Canadian author, educator, and eighth president of the University of Toronto.

187. Henry Ford: American industrialist, and founder of the Ford Motor Company.

188. Sanaya Roman: Author of *Living with Joy: Keys to Personal Power and Spiritual Transformation*

189. Albert Schweitzer: He was a theologian, organist, writer, humanitarian, philosopher, and physician.

190. Richard Branson: is an English business magnate, investor, author and philanthropist.

191. Kat Cole: American businesswoman. She is the Chief operating officer and president of North America for Focus Brands. She is a former president of Cinnabon.

192. Elon Musk: is a business magnate, industrial designer, engineer, and philanthropist. He is the founder, CEO, CTO and chief designer of SpaceX; CEO and product architect of Tesla, Inc.

193. Watts Wacker, Jim Taylor and Howard Means: authors of *The Visionary's Handbook*.

194. Joe Rogan: comedian, podcast host, actor, television host, and mixed martial arts commentator.

195. Grant Cardone: internationally-renowned speaker on sales, leadership, real estate investing, entrepreneurship and finance.

196. Travis Bradberry: the co-author of Emotional Intelligence 2.0 and co-founder of TalentSmart, a San Diego provider of emotional intelligence tests and training, serving more than 75 percent of Fortune 500 companies.

197. Harry S. Truman: was the 33rd president of the United States from 1945 to 1953.

198. Anita Roddick: was a British businesswoman, human rights activist and environmental campaigner, best known as the founder of The Body Shop.

199. Lolly Daskal: the founder of Lead from Within, a global leadership, executive coaching, and consulting firm based in New York City. Author of *The Leadership Gap: What Gets Between You and Your Greatness*

200. James Buchanan: was an American lawyer and politician who served as the 15th president of the United States.

201. Reverend Theodore Hesburgh: became an ordained priest of the Congregation of Holy Cross and is best known for his service as the president of the University of Notre Dame.

202. John Doerr: is an American investor and venture capitalist at Kleiner Perkins.

203. Mike Abrashoff: Former Commander, USS Benfold and Author, *It's Your Ship.*

204. Tom Brady: American football quarterback, winning 6 Super Bowls with the New England Patriots.

205. James Kouzes and Barry Posner: authors of *The Leadership Challenge.*

206. Steve Jobs: was an American entrepreneur best known as the co-founder, chairman, and CEO of Apple Inc.

207. Arnold Schwarzenegger: Austrian-American actor, businessman, former politician and professional bodybuilder. He served as the 38th Governor of California from 2003 to 2011.

208. George S. Patton: was a general of the United States Army who commanded the U.S. Seventh Army in the Mediterranean theater of World War II, and the U.S. Third Army in France and Germany after the Allied invasion of Normandy in June 1944.

209. Warren Bennis: was an American scholar, organizational consultant and author, widely regarded as a pioneer of the contemporary field of Leadership studies.

210. Daisaku Ikeda: is a Japanese Buddhist philosopher, educator, author, and nuclear disarmament advocate.

211. Sir William Osler: was a Canadian physician and one of the four founding professors of Johns Hopkins Hospital.

212. Claude M. Bristol: was a lawyer, lecturer, investment banker, and foreign correspondent. He is the coauthor of the long-time bestseller, "TNT: The Power Within.

213. Jim Collins: is an American researcher, author, speaker and consultant focused on the subject of business management and company sustainability and growth.

214. Pope Paul VI: was head of the Catholic Church and

sovereign of the Vatican City State from 21 June 1963 to his death in 1978.

215. John C. Maxwell: an American author, speaker, and pastor who has written many books, primarily focusing on leadership. Titles nclude: *The 21 Irrefutable Laws of Leadership* and *The 21 Indispensable Qualities of a Leader.*

216. Elon Musk: is a business magnate, industrial designer, engineer, and philanthropist. He is the founder, CEO, CTO and chief designer of SpaceX; CEO and product architect of Tesla, Inc.

217. Arnold Schwarzenegger: Austrian-American actor, businessman, former politician and professional bodybuilder. He served as the 38th Governor of California from 2003 to 2011.

218. Jocko Willink: a retired U.S. Navy SEAL officer, co-author of the #1 New York Times bestseller *Extreme Ownership: How U.S. Navy SEALs Lead and Win, Dichotomy of Leadership,* Podcast host, and co-founder of Echelon Front.

219. Helen Keller: was an American author, political activist, and lecturer. She was the first deaf-blind person to earn a Bachelor of Arts degree.

220. Tony Dorsett: is a former American football running back who played professionally in the National Football League (NFL) for the Dallas Cowboys and Denver Broncos.

221. Kathleen Schafer: author of *Living The Leadership Choice,* learn more at kathleenschafer.com

222. Ken Blanchard: has influenced the day-to-day management and leadership of people and companies throughout the world. His most successful book, The One Minute Manager, has sold over 13 million copies. Learn more at www.kenblanchard.com

223. James Kouzes and Barry Posner: authors of *The Leadership Challenge.*

224. Gloria Steinem: is an American feminist, journalist, and social political activist who became nationally recognized as a leader and a spokeswoman for the American feminist movement in the late 1960s and early 1970s.

225. Milton Berle: was an American comedian and actor. His career as an entertainer spanned over 80 years, first in silent films and on stage as a child actor, then in radio, movies and television.

226. Grace Hansen: I've come across this quote in several places attributing it to Grace Hansen, but unfortunately I could not find any reliable information about this person.

227. Peter Diamandis: is a Greek American engineer, physician, and entrepreneur best known for being founder and chairman of the X Prize Foundation.

228. Dale Carnegie: author of *How to Win Friends and Influence People*. He was a writer, lecturer, and developer of self-improvement courses. Learn more at www.dalecarnegie.com

229. Irene Rosenfield: was the chairman and chief executive officer of Mondelēz International.

230. Thomas Jefferson: was an American statesman, diplomat, lawyer, architect, philosopher, and Founding Father who served as the third president of the United States from 1801 to 1809.

231. Michael Jordan: former professional basketball player and the principal owner of the Charlotte Hornets. He played 15 seasons in the NBA, winning six championships with the Chicago Bulls. considered by many to be the greatest basketball player of all time.

232. Steve Jobs: was an American entrepreneur best known as the co-founder, chairman, and CEO of Apple Inc.

233. Deepak Chopra: an Indian-American author and alternative-medicine advocate. His books and videos have made him one of the best-known and wealthiest figures in alternative medicine.

234. Joe Namath: nicknamed "Broadway Joe", is an American former professional football player who was a quarterback in the American Football League and National Football League during the 1960s and 1970s.

235. Gary Vaynerchuk: entrepreneur, New York Times bestselling author, speaker, and Internet personality.

236. Rachel Hollis

237. Leo Buscaglia: also known as "Dr. Love," was an American author and motivational speaker, and a professor at the University of Southern California.

238. Simon Sinek: a British-born American author and motivational speaker. He is the author of five books, including *Start With Why*.

239. Captain David Marquet: retired from the Navy in 2009 and is now the author of *Turn the Ship Around! A True Story of Turning Followers Into Leaders*.

240. Ray Dalio: an American billionaire hedge fund manager and philanthropist who has served as co-chief investment officer of Bridgewater Associates since 1985. Author of *Principles: Life and Work*.

241. Jesse Jackson: an American civil rights activist, Baptist minister, and politician. He was a candidate for the Democratic presidential nomination in 1984 and 1988.

242. Vince Lombardi: best known as the head coach of the Green Bay Packers during the 1960s. He led them to victory in the first two Super Bowls. Learn more www.vincelombardi.com

243. Vesta Kelly: I've come across this quote in several places attributing it to Vesta Kelly, but unfortunately I could not find any reliable information about this person.

244. Bene Brown: an American professor, lecturer, author, and podcast host. Author of *Dare To Lead*.

245. Aldous Huxley: was an English writer and philosopher. He wrote nearly fifty books, as well as wide-ranging essays, narratives, and poems. Author of *Brave New World* and *The Perennial Philosophy*.

246. Larry Page: an American software engineer and Internet entrepreneur. He is best known as one of the co-founders of Google.

247. Elon Musk: is a business magnate, industrial designer, engineer, and philanthropist. He is the founder, CEO, CTO and chief designer of SpaceX; CEO and product architect of Tesla, Inc.

248. John C. Maxwell: an American author, speaker, and pastor who has written many books, primarily focusing on leadership. Titles include: *The 21 Irrefutable Laws of Leadership* and *The 21 Indispensable Qualities of a Leader*.

249. Abraham Lincoln: was an American statesman and lawyer who served as the 16th president of the United States from 1861 to 1865.

250. Mark Twain: Samuel Langhorne Clemens, known by his pen name Mark Twain, was an American writer, humorist, entrepreneur, publisher, and lecturer. He was lauded as the

"greatest humorist [the United States] has produced",
251. Unknown
252. Anthony Robbins: one of the biggest names in the self-help field. Robbins helps people transform the quality of their lives, become better leaders, and reach peak performance. To learn more visit his website www.tonyrobbins.com
253. Ronald Heifetz: is among the world's foremost authorities on the practice and teaching of leadership. He speaks extensively and advises heads of governments, businesses, and nonprofit organizations across the globe.
254. Diana Ross: an American singer and actress. She rose to fame as the lead singer of The Supremes, one of the world's best-selling girl groups of all time.
255. Bernard Montgomery: was a senior British Army officer who served in both the First World War and the Second World War.
256. Christine Lagarde (International Monetary Fund)
257. Henna Inam: author of *Wired for Authenticity: Seven Practices to Inspire, Adapt, & Lead*
258. Robert Hughes: was an Australian-born art critic, writer, and producer of television documentaries. He was described as "the most famous art critic in the world."
259. Dali Lama: The 14th Dalai Lama of Tibetan Buddhism.
260. Brian Tracy: a self-help author, motivational speaker, and business coach. Learn more at www.briantracy.com
261. Kahlil Gibran: Lebanese-American artist, writer, and poet. He's most famous for his 1923 book *The Prophet*.
262. Norman Vincent Peale: minister, proponent of positive thinking, and author of *The Power of Positive Thinking*.
263. Theodore Roosevelt: an American statesman, politician, conservationist, naturalist, and writer, who served as the 26th president of the United States.
264. Richard Bach: an American writer widely known as the author of some of the 1970s' biggest sellers, including *Jonathan Livingston Seagull* and *Illusions: The Adventures of a Reluctant Messiah*.
265. Anatole France: was a French poet, journalist, and novelist with several best-sellers.
266. Basil King: was a Canadian clergyman who became a

writer after retiring from the clergy.

267. Mahatma Gandhi: preeminent leader of Indian nationalism in British-ruled India, employing non-violent civil disobedience. He led India to independence and inspired movements for non-violence, civil rights, and freedom across the world.

268. Eleanor Roosevelt: wife of President Franklin D. Roosevelt. She was an advocate for civil rights, an international author, speaker, and politician.

269. Hal Elrod: an American author, keynote speaker and success coach. He is the author of the bestselling books *The Miracle Morning* and *The Miracle Equation*.

270. Timothy Ferriss: podcaster, investor, and author of: *The 4-Hour Workweek, The 4-Hour Body, The 4-Hour Chef, Tools of Titans, and Tribe of Mentors*.

271. Peter Drucker: Austrian-born American management consultant, educator, and author.

272. Richard Branson: is an English business magnate, investor, author and philanthropist.

273. Deepak Chopra: an Indian-American author and alternative-medicine advocate. His books and videos have made him one of the best-known and wealthiest figures in alternative medicine.

274. Michael Jordan: former professional basketball player and the principal owner of the Charlotte Hornets. He played 15 seasons in the NBA, winning six championships with the Chicago Bulls. considered by many to be the greatest basketball player of all time.

275. W. Clement Stone: was a businessman, philanthropist and New Thought self-help book author.

276. George Bernard Shaw: was an Irish playwright, critic, polemicist and political activist. His influence on Western theatre, culture and politics extended from the 1880s to his death and beyond.

277. Tommy Lasorda: an American former Major League Baseball pitcher, coach, and manager, who is best known for his two decades managing the Los Angeles Dodgers

278. Peter Marshall: an American game show host, television and radio personality, singer, and actor. He was the original host of The Hollywood Squares

279. Sharon Adler: is an inspirational author. Her tidbits of wisdom have been published in over 100 different books.
280. Jack Ma: is a Chinese business magnate, investor and philanthropist. He is the co-founder and former executive chairman of Alibaba Group.
281. John Calvin Coolidge: was an American politician and lawyer who served as the 30th president of the United States
282. Emma Watson: is an English actress, model, and activist.
283. Joe Tichio: author, chiropractor, businessman.
284. Travis Bradberry: the co-author of Emotional Intelligence 2.0 and co-founder of TalentSmart, a San Diego provider of emotional intelligence tests and training, serving more than 75 percent of Fortune 500 companies. @talentsmarteq.
285. Bible, Galatians 6:9
286. A. Lou Vickery: is a former professional baseball player and speaker/trainer.
287. Grant Cardone: internationally-renowned speaker on sales, leadership, real estate investing, entrepreneurship and finance.
288. Simon Sinek: a British-born American author and motivational speaker. He is the author of five books, including *Start With Why*.
289. Vivian Greene: was a British writer regarded as the world's foremost expert on dolls' houses. She was also the widow of the distinguished novelist Graham Greene.
290. Thich Nhat Hanh: is a Vietnamese Thiền Buddhist monk, peace activist, and founder of the Plum Village Tradition.
291. Lisa Cash Hanson: blogger, marketer, spokesperson, and CEO of Snugwugg Inc.
292. Beverly Sills: was an American operatic soprano.
293. Dale Carnegie: author of *How to Win Friends and Influence People*. He was a writer, lecturer, and developer of self-improvement courses. Learn more www.dalecarnegie.com
294. Seth Godin: American entrepreneur, author, and speaker. Learn more at www.sethgodin.com
295. Larry Page: an American software engineer and Internet entrepreneur. He is best known as one of the co-founders of Google.
296. Antoine de Saint-Exupery: was a French writer, poet, aristocrat, journalist and pioneering aviator.

297. Unknown

298. Robert Greene: an American author known for his books on strategy, power, and seduction. He has written six international bestsellers: *The 48 Laws of Power, The Art of Seduction, The 33 Strategies of War, The 50th Law, Mastery, and The Laws of Human Nature.*

299. Stephen R. Covey: American educator, author, speaker, and businessman. His most popular book was *The Seven Habits of Highly Effective People.* Learn more www.stephencovey.com

300. Norman Schwarzkopf: was a United States Army general. While serving as the commander of United States Central Command, he led all coalition forces in the Gulf War.

301. Rabbi Harold Kushner: a prominent American rabbi and a popular author.

302. J. Carla Nortcutt: a seminary professor.

303. Max DePree: best known for his work as the CEO of Herman Miller, Inc.

304. Euripides: he is one of the three ancient Greek tragedians for whom any plays have survived in full.

305. Frances Hesselbein: is the former CEO of the Girl Scouts of the USA, from 1976 to 1990, and is the president and CEO of the Frances Hesselbein Leadership Forum.

306. William Cohen: author of *The Stuff of Heroes: The Eight Universal Laws of Leadership.*

307. William Arthur Ward: author of more than 100 articles, poems and meditations published in such magazines as Reader's Digest, The Phi Delta Kappan, Science of Mind, and various Christian publications.

308. James E. Faust: was an American religious leader, lawyer, and politician.

309. Sheila Murray Bethel: is a successful entrepreneur, best selling author and a hall-of-fame keynote speaker.

310. Dr. Susan Madsen: is a sought-after speaker in local, national, and international settings.

311. General Colin Powell: an American politician, diplomat and retired four-star general who served as the 65th United States Secretary of State from 2001 to 2005. Author of several books on leadership.

312. Arnold Schwarzenegger: Austrian-American actor,

businessman, former politician and professional bodybuilder. He served as the 38th Governor of California from 2003 to 2011.

313. Friedrich Nietzsche: was a German philosopher, cultural critic, composer, poet, and philologist whose work has exerted a profound influence on modern intellectual history.

314. Ralph Waldo Emerson: American essayist, lecturer, and poet who led the Transcendentalist movement in the mid 19th century. He is most famous for *Self-Reliance*, *The American Scholar*, and *Nature*.

315. George Washington: was an American political leader, military general, statesman, and Founding Fath.er who served as the first president of the United States

316. Warren Bennis: was an American scholar, organizational consultant and author, widely regarded as a pioneer of the contemporary field of Leadership studies.

317. Jim Mattis: a retired United States Marine Corps general who served as the 26th US secretary of defense from January 2017 through January 2019. Author of *Call Sign Chaos: Learning to Lead*.

318. Dan Millman: is an American author and lecturer in the personal development field. He is best-known for his book *Way Of The Peaceful Warrior*.

319. Howard Schultz: American businessman. He served as the chairman and chief executive officer of the Starbucks Coffee Company from 1986 to 2000, and then again from 2008 to 2017.

320. Mother Teresa: honored in the Catholic Church as Saint Teresa of Calcutta, was an Albanian-Indian Roman Catholic nun and missionary.

321. Gary Vaynerchuk: entrepreneur, New York Times bestselling author, speaker, and Internet personality.

322. Leo Buscaglia: also known as "Dr. Love," was an American author and motivational speaker, and a professor at the University of Southern California.

323. Unknown

324. Napoleon Hill: American self-help author of *Think and Grow Rich* which is among the 10 best selling self-help books of all time.

325. John D. Rockefeller: was an American business magnate and philanthropist. He is widely considered the wealthiest

American of all time, and the richest person in modern history.

326. Muhammad Ali: was an American professional boxer, activist, and philanthropist. Nicknamed "The Greatest"

327. Herbert B. Swope: was a U.S. editor, journalist and intimate of the Algonquin Round Table.

328. Reed Markham: is the author of books such as Excellence In Public Speaking.

329. Dwight D. Eisenhower: American politician and soldier who served as the 34th president of the United States from 1953 to 1961.

330. J.K. Rowling: is best known for writing the Harry Potter fantasy series, which has won multiple awards and sold more than 500 million copies, becoming the best-selling book series in history.

331. Chuck Swindoll: evangelical Christian pastor, author, and educator. Learn more by visiting www.insight.org.

332. Howard Schultz: American businessman. He served as the chairman and chief executive officer of the Starbucks Coffee Company from 1986 to 2000, and then again from 2008 to 2017.

333. Alan Mulally: is an American aerospace engineer and manufacturing executive. He is the former President and Chief Executive Officer of the Ford Motor Company.

334. Arnold Glasow: Author of *Glasow's Gloombusters*.

335. Richard Branson: is an English business magnate, investor, author and philanthropist.

336. Roy T. Bennett: author of The Light in the Heart. He loves sharing positive thoughts and creative insight.

337. Joe DiMaggio: nicknamed "Joltin' Joe" and "The Yankee Clipper", was an American baseball center fielder who played his entire 13-year career in Major League Baseball for the New York Yankees.

338. Robin S. Sharma: a Canadian writer, best known for his *The Monk Who Sold His Ferrari* book series.

339. Winston Churchill: was a British statesman, army officer, and writer. He was Prime Minister of the United Kingdom from 1940 to 1945, when he led the country to victory in the Second World War.

340. Sylvester Stallone: is an American actor, director, screenwriter, and producer most famous for the *Rocky* movies.

341. Audre Lorde: Caribbean-American writer, poet, and activist.

342. Khalil Gibran: Lebanese-American artist, writer, and poet. He's most famous for his 1923 book *The Prophet*.

343. Wilma Mankiller: was a Cherokee activist, social worker, community developer and the first woman elected to serve as Principal Chief of the Cherokee Nation.

344. John F. Kennedy: served as the 35th president of the United States.

345. Dr. Seuss: Theodor Seuss "Ted" Geisel was an American children's author, political cartoonist, illustrator, poet, animator, screenwriter, and filmmaker.

346. Seneca: was a Hispano-Roman Stoic philosopher, statesman, dramatist, and satirist from the Silver Age of Latin literature.

347. Patrick Bet-David: is a successful startup entrepreneur, CEO of PHP Agency, Inc., author and Creator of Valuetainment.

348. Lao Tzu: philosopher of ancient China and best known as the author of the Tao Te Ching, a fundamental text of Taoism.

349. Warren Bennis: was an American scholar, organizational consultant and author, widely regarded as a pioneer of the contemporary field of Leadership studies.

350. Benjamin Franklin: was one of the Founding Fathers of the United States. Franklin was a leading writer, printer, political philosopher, politician, Freemason, postmaster, scientist, inventor, humorist, civic activist, statesman, and diplomat.

351. Leo Buscaglia: also known as "Dr. Love," was an American author and motivational speaker, and a professor at the University of Southern California.

352. Roopleen Prasad: is a Motivational Counselor, Speaker, blogger, life enthusiast, author of 4 books and has contributed to many anthologies. Learn more at www.drroopleen.com

353. Isaac Newton: was an English mathematician, physicist, astronomer, theologian, and author who is widely recognized as one of the most influential scientists of all time.

354. Sam Altman: is an American entrepreneur, investor, programmer, and blogger.

355. Khalil Gibran: Lebanese-American artist, writer, and poet. He's most famous for his 1923 book *The Prophet*.

356. Brandon Sanderson
357. Gary Vaynerchuk: entrepreneur, New York Times bestselling author, speaker, and Internet personality.
358. Joel Brown: author, speaker and coach. Find out more at www.iamjoelbrown.com
359. William Arthur Ward: author of more than 100 articles, poems and meditations published in such magazines as Reader's Digest, The Phi Delta Kappan, Science of Mind, and various Christian publications.
360. Max DePree: best known for his work as the CEO of Herman Miller, Inc.
361. Jocko Willink: a retired U.S. Navy SEAL officer, co-author of the #1 New York Times bestseller *Extreme Ownership: How U.S. Navy SEALs Lead and Win*, *Dichotomy of Leadership*, Podcast host, and co-founder of Echelon Front.
362. Tony Robbins: one of the biggest names in the self help field. Robbins helps people transform the quality of their lives, become better leaders, and reach peak performance. To learn more visit his website www.tonyrobbins.com
363. Amelia Earhart: was an American aviation pioneer and the first female aviator to fly solo across the Atlantic Ocean.
364. Toni Morrison: was an American novelist, essayist, book editor, and college professor.
365. Travis Bradberry: the co-author of Emotional Intelligence 2.0 and co-founder of TalentSmart, a San Diego provider of emotional intelligence tests and training, serving more than 75 percent of Fortune 500 companies.

ABOUT THE AUTHOR

Joe Tichio is the author of Greatest Inspirational Quotes and Greatest Leadership Quotes. Since 2008, he has been sharing inspiration online, as a speaker, and through his books. He is happily married to his beautiful wife, and they have 2 amazing daughters. He is an entrepreneur, chiropractor, and advocate for healthy living.